THE MOON RISES OVER ISALE EKO

Ahmed Koroma

Sierra Leonean Writers Series

The Moon Rises Over Isale Eko

ISBN: 978-99910-54-61-2

Sierra Leonean Writers Series
120 Kissy Road, Freetown; Warima,
Sierra Leone
Publisher: Prof. Osman Sankoh (Mallam O.)
www.sl-writers-series.org

He sprinkles millets and tosses goat horns
dead at dawn

And with his umbilical cord fastened tightly
around his neck
he lies prostrate

at the crossroads where four roads meet
where the moon crosses path with the sun...

...the moon that rises over Isale Eko
once again

We shall not cease from exploration
And the end of all our exploring
Will be to arrive where we started
And know the place for the first time.
Through the unknown, unremembered gate
When the last of earth left to discover
Is that which was the beginning;
At the source of the longest river
The voice of the hidden waterfall
And the children in the apple-tree

T.S. Eliot. The Gidding.

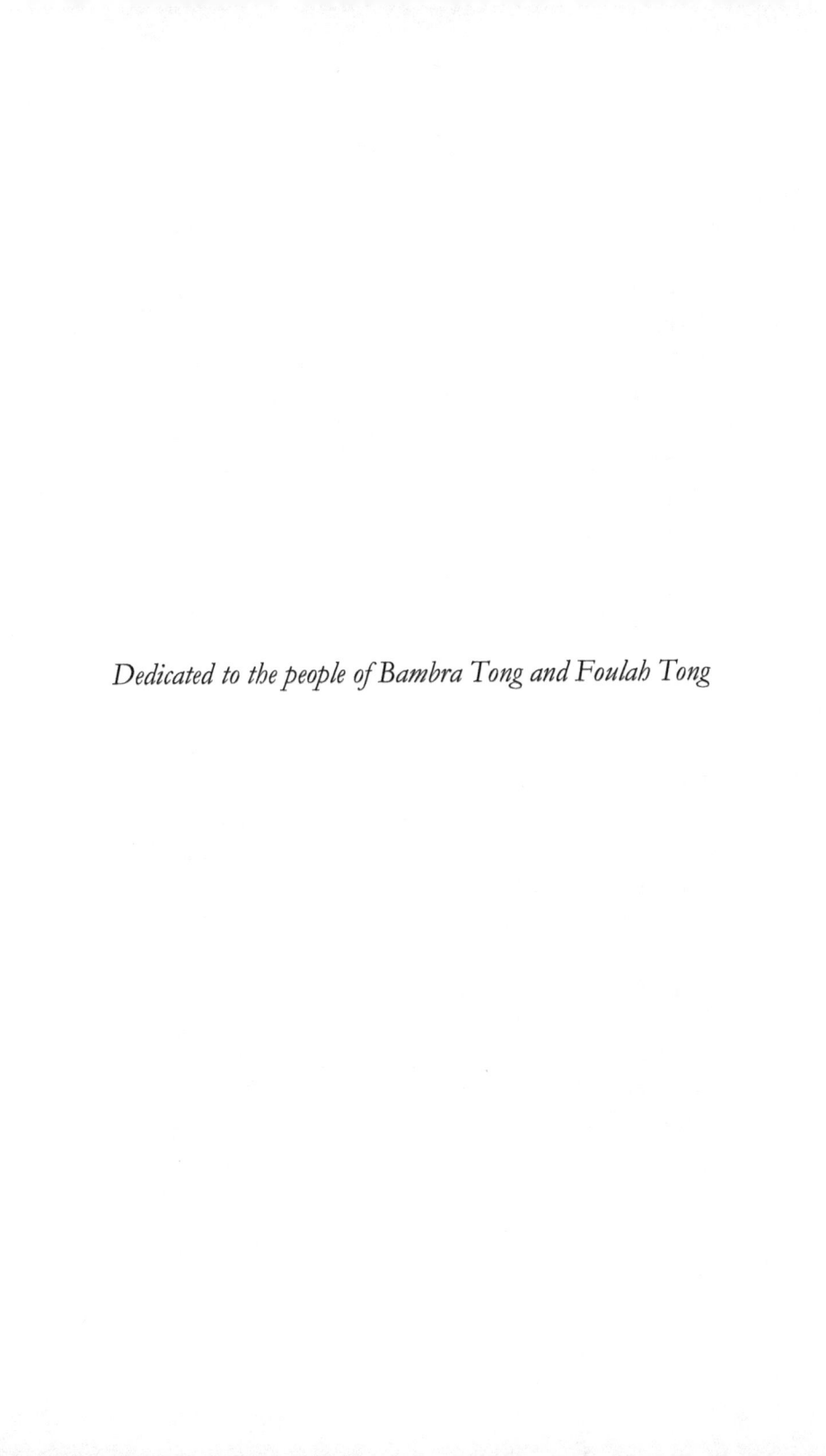

Dedicated to the people of Bambra Tong and Foulah Tong

Table of Contents

Time Travel in a Broken Canoe

Foreword by

Abdul Tejan-Cole

Very often, I am asked by friends and colleagues who are planning to visit Sierra Leone to recommend a good travel guide that they can read before their trip. I have embarrassingly always struggled as none of the current books I have seen provide an accurate picture of what to expect. Most fall very short, whilst others talk about a Sierra Leone I do not recognize. They are mostly written by 'experts' who barely spend a few weeks or months in the country.

As I read Ahmed 'Stokes' Koroma's third collection of poems, it occurred to me that I may have been looking at the wrong section of the bookshop or shelf for a book to recommend. Until now, it had never occurred to me that a collection of poems could be the best travelogue – the best and most useful source of information of our home town, Freetown, and *Sweet Salone* as we fondly call our native land.

There is no better person than Ahmed Koroma to write about Freetown in particular. He knows the city inside out. He was born, grew up and educated in the city. He calls the environs around Regent Road, Circular Road, Sackville Street, Mountain Cut and the entire *Bambra Tong, Foulah Tong, Magazine* and *Fourah Bay* communities in the central and east end parts of Freetown his home. But his knowledge of the city transcends far beyond those communities. Like myself, he attended school at Kingtom in west end Freetown. He got the

1

early stages of his secondary education - Forms one to five - at St Edwards Secondary School before crossing the road to the Prince of Wales School for his Sixth form. It was the opposite in my case. Afterwards, both of us ended up at Fourah Bay College, Mount Aureol. Whilst he opted to study atoms, I chose to delve into the minefield called law.

'The Moon Rises Over Isale Eko' is the perfect tool for anyone keen to know the real Sierra Leone. It gives a vivid and unflinchingly accurate account of the author's country of birth. The anthology sparked nostalgic feelings of the reflective type. Though bittersweet, I never wanted the feeling to fade. He reminisces about the good and hard life in the land that he loves. The book correctly captures the good, the bad and the ugly of Sierra Leone. Ahmed Koroma's memory is vivid and uplifting. It describes local events, places, games, lores, traditions, etc. with as such clear and sensory details that it brings back fond memories of growing up in this city - a longing to return to those days. The collection of poems is not just for intending visitors to Sierra Leone. It serves as an excellent tool to help educate young Sierra Leoneans about life in their country in decades gone by and hopefully be a source of hope and inspiration. For middle aged and older Sierra Leoneans, it will regurgitate fond memories of yesteryears.

Like his previous collections, 'Of Flour and Tears' and "Along the Odokoko River", the poems in this collection are contemplative. For some, they may evoke sad, somber and solemn emotions. For a true native, they resonate and inspire hope and a longing – a yearning to return home even though times are much tougher and harder now. Though he emigrated to the United States in 1991 and lives in the comfy trend-setting metropolis that is Los Angeles, he continues to maintain an intimate relationship with his country of birth. This staunch love and care for his native land comes out clearly in all his poems.

His return to the land that he loves is inevitable. The very first poem "Freetown", about our home town starts with the line *'when I return to you.'* It is not If I return to you. He seeks to return to the Freetown of his childhood – the "authentic" Freetown.

'So, do not paint the trunks of trees
nor whitewash the cemetery walls
I do not want to be welcomed
with buntings, flags on crisscross wires
on steel poles and wooden fences.'

That is the fake Freetown we create for dignitaries and other visitors. It is not the Freetown we know. He seeks the Freetown with no fanfare and with no Mayor wearing regalia.

'I want to be greeted by gentle fumes
the smell of hot pepper soup on concrete
mixed with odor of decayed compost
sewage rats and roaming pigs
I love you for who you are
and for who you once were.'

Despite all the decadence. Yes, the rats in the sewage, the roaming pigs in Freetown's slums. That is the Freetown he seeks to be greeted by.

The genuine authentic Freetown. His true love. His heart.

'Do not bake rice bread
and sweet ginger cakes for me
let me dip my hands in palm oil soup
and slimy intestines.
I fell in love with you
when your roads were deserted and blue
and I still do
so, when I return to you
I want to see faces old and new.'

He doesn't want to eat from plates; no he prefers the stainless-steel bowls we were accustomed to as kids in the east end of Freetown. He opts for the *Bubu Gang* instead of any local artiste aping western musicians. Even with the local cuisine he is very choosy; not rice bread of ginger cake but a sauce with palm oil overflowing and the slimy intestines usually of cows aplenty. Yummy.

He reminisces about our childhood days when as little kids who took fun and delight in tapping the leaves of the *Mimosa pudica* (sensitive mimosa), plant whose compound leaves fold inward and droop when touched or shaken, defending themselves from harm, and re-open a few minutes later. As the leaves fold, we chant *"tie you lappa you man dae cam.'*

Like most of us, the author is passionately in love with his home town,

'You were a picturesque town
and your beauty still shines
through the blemishes of yesteryears.

*Illuminate the sea with that radiant smile
that reminds me of your lush greenery
now mixed with red clay and grime
that seem to dampen your spirit.*

*But your essence remains strong
you are a town of every kind
of every hereditary bloodline.'*

And concludes with the stanza,

*'You are my favorite town
my hamlet by the sea
you set me free
to roam the distant lands
and I am returning to you.'*

This is the Freetown I know, and I love. The city leased from the natives that became home for freed slaves and Recaptives. Long after it was set up as part of the realm of the free, it continues to set many of its sons and daughters like the author free.

The entire collection is well armed with rich and powerful images of childhood memories. The author aptly captures his childhood odyssey. The beautiful games of hopscotch or as we call it locally *'ah die.'* The egret on top of a grazing cow feeding on crickets, butterflies and moths after the rain. Enjoying the wavy sound of the blue water as he sits by the seashore. Building on the famous Krio proverb, 'a broken canoe in a wharf belongs to someone', he writes about a broken canoe that is hopeful of 'flying' away when the tropical storm returns. Even in faraway Ciudad Juarez, he longs for

'that faraway town
where she buried a white cowry
and a withered plant…'

The Ghanaian author Ayei Kwei Armah had written that the beautyful ones are not yet born. Playing on this, in a poem titled 'A Beautyful One', Ahmed Koroma describes the birth of a child *'with poetry tattooed on her forehead.'* Despite hearing

'…..the call
of a hopeless society
of those that creep
through stained barbed wires
to fend for stale crumbs
and fragments of wheat
on the other side of the hill'

the child still leaps out from the belly of *Yemoja*, the motherly Yoruba water god who cures infertility and is strongly protective, and cares deeply for all her children, comforting them and cleansing them of sorrow, *grabbing her crystalline beads on her way out.* Is she the beautyful one? The one who brings salvation to the land? Our guardian of progressive transformation? The poem leaves us guessing.

Like in his previous collections, this book is replete with references to Nigerian words and terms. In addition to the Yoruba God, *Yemoja*, reference is also made to *Ogun*, the orisha, spirit or god of war, iron, metals, tools and weapons. *Ogun* is said to be the father of civilization and first appeared

6

as a fierce warrior named *Tobe Ode*. He is said to have been the first Orisha to descend to the realm of *Ile Aiye* ("Earth"), to find suitable place for future human life. Other references are made to the *uko* tree known to some as the *ikoro* tree or *oji* wood (Chlorophora excelsa). This tree is very symbolic as it is believed to have supernatural powers. Many West African proverbs make references to this tree - The lizard that jumped from the high *iroko* tree said he would praise himself if no one else did; We live by hope, but a seed never becomes an *iroko* tree by dreaming and it is from a small seed that the giant *iroko* tree has its beginning. *Ago-go*, the Yoruba word for bell is also mentioned as is *ile aiye*, a Yoruba word meaning earth or this world.

These references highlight the link and close connection between Sierra Leone and Nigeria. Freetown was home for the Recaptives or Liberated Africans - slaves who had been captured but never made it to Europe or the Americas. Many of those captured were Yorubas and Igbos from Nigeria. They brought with them their culture, traditions, names etc. and it became integrated as part of the culture of people of Freetown who have since the 1800s been referred to by various names such as Krios, Aku Krios, Kossoh Krios, Oku etc. Ahmed Koroma grew up in these communities and it is for this reason that in his poems, he makes regular reference to Yoruba gods and expressions.

The collection of poems does not eulogize Sierra Leone. Where necessary it is unforgiving and boldly critical. The infuriation trilogy in the anthology highlights lost opportunities. Opportunities which angers and exasperates the author. The hope of the nation gone wrong. Mount Aureol, where the oldest western style college in sub-Saharan Africa, Fourah Bay College, is situated is;

"the apathy of the educated few
The religiosity and feign optimism
And the calculated rationale of the elites"

Ahmed Koroma reserves his harshest language and shows his exasperation as he describes

'It is the noxious fumes suffocating the masses
Emitting from the flatulent exhaust of pigs
Parading the streets amid zombies and robots
...
It is the futility of hope, of courage betrayed'

It infuriates the crap out of him. Pademba Road, where the central prison is located, and Marbella, a slum settlement, do the same to him. The latter is the complete opposite and a far cry from the other Marbella, the chic, sun-drenched holiday resort in the Costa del Sol in Malaga, Spain. Freetown's Marbella is filled with broken bottles, fecal mess, carcasses of salmonella laden fowls. The author is angered by

'The negligence, the apathy and greed
Of those who plant seeds that refuse to grow
And insist we wait for many moons to show
It is the deliberateness of their inaction
That infuriates the crap out of me.'

But the collection of poems is overwhelmingly positive and sanguine. Many of the positives pop out in different parts of the collection.

Much has been written and said about religious harmony and tolerance in Sierra Leone. Christians and Muslims living together peacefully, sharing food and gifts with each other during religious festivals and in some cases even inter marrying. Many of my Christian friends can recite the first chapter (surah) in the Holy Quran, Sūrat al-Fātihah and I often heard stories of Muslim students topping their Bible study classes. This harmony is evident in this collection. One moment, the author is describing the struggles of a muezzin to wake up and do the morning call for prayer, a regular event on a Freetown morning. In the next poem, he credits the *'pastor at the church with the stained glass the one who taught us to scream hallelujah and then traded our effigy for a tiny cross'* from saving his brother with the paper boat from the liquid spirit.

American psychologist and author, Laurie Anne Helgoe is quoted to have said that "Reading is like travel, allowing you to exit your own life for a bit, and to come back with a renewed, even inspired, perspective." In reading this anthology, Ahmed 'Stokes' Koroma not only took me back home, he took me back in time. The simplicity of the language made the poems very easy to read and understand. True, without background and context some of the poems may not be easily or fully understood. Yet the descriptive nature will leave the reader with a clear sense of the message being conveyed. Let's hope it will entice many to visit our lovely country and help bring back fond memories.

Freetown

"Of all the years I ever knew
Those finer ones I spent with you" — David Gates

Dear Freetown

When I return to you
I do not expect a delirious mask
nor the pretense of a blissful town
rather it is the authentic you
the battle scars down your tired face
reminding me of your stunning past.

When I return to you
I want to be greeted by gentle fumes
the smell of hot pepper soup on concrete
mixed with odor of decayed compost
sewage rats and roaming pigs
I love you for who you are
and for who you once were.

So, do not paint the trunks of trees
nor whitewash the cemetery walls
I do not want to be welcomed
with buntings, flags on crisscross wires
on steel poles and wooden fences.

Place my picture next to the woman
who spits at passersby
in broad daylight.
Let her scream my name out loud

as my vehicle gallops through a heap
of dirty rags.

Let the mayor not wear a broad
medallion, and tassel of many colors
and the bishop his *Mitra Pretiosa*.
Let the priest sprinkle holy water
at the doorstep of the tabernacle
across where statues once stood.

When I return to you
I want the imam to read *surat ul naas*
to remind me of my battles with rats
deep in the abyss of the odokoko.
I want him to scream the *azan*
atop of that grassy hill
where we used to herd sheep.

Do not bake rice bread
and sweet ginger cakes for me.
Let me dip my hands in palm oil soup
and slimy intestines.

I fell in love with you
when your roads were deserted and blue
and I still do.
So, when I return to you
I want to see faces old and new.

Bring out the drums,
the stainless-steel bowls.
Let the girl with bells on her toes
and the boy who walks on stilts

tap every *touch-me-not* plant
along the bushy path.
Let the leaves tie their *lapa*
before their husbands arrive.

Let the boy who plucks cocoyam leaves
to shield from the inclined rain
roll his bicycle rim down narrow streets.

Hang colorful *fanoos* on every porch.
Let the griot serenade me with melody
and the prophet who speak in tongues
predict the next firestorm.

Elevate the houses made of wood
on pillars, high into the folding clouds.
Raise the window blinds way higher
exposing the curtains with rainbow colors.

You were a picturesque town
and your beauty still shines
through the blemishes of yesteryears.

Illuminate the sea with that radiant smile
that reminds me of your lush greenery,
now mixed with red clay and grime
that seem to dampen your spirit.

But your essence remains strong
you are a town of every kind
of every hereditary bloodline.

Commission the *Bubu* Gang
to play rhythm for women
and men in a soulful trance.
Bring out the two-headed king
the one who raises his staff
to ward off evil spirits.

Let the pedestrians skip puddles
after a rainy night,
the mango flies and mosquitos

compete for my ears.

Witness the overflowing stream
emptying into the bursting bay.
Observe the foam drifting down
from the brook where girls wash clothes.
I will follow the drifting debris
to the waterfall underneath the bridge.

Remove the *never-die* leaf
hidden within the crumpled pages
of the old bible at the chapel,
and read the inscription of the past.

Bring out the pots and pans
as we gaze at the lunar eclipse,
and wake me up from a stupor
so I can listen to the old woman
passionately pleading to *yankuba*
to save us from perpetual darkness.

I return to you
to read poetry at the bandstand
where we used to do improve
and chew cassava and groundnut.
It is the voice of the unknown
the evoking sound of the hunter's flute
that entice me back to you.

You are my favorite town
my hamlet by the sea
you set me free
to roam the distant lands
and I am returning to you.

Road to Jange

It is with mixed feeling
with hope and despair
that I take this journey
down this road of recollections
to the place where buffalos roam

The ragged old truck blows dust
into my eyes, and the unbearable sun
melts my melanin pigment away

Tinkonko, Bumpeh, Sembehun, Serabu
Motuo, Bauya, Semabu, Luawa,

Boulders and potholes, an assemblage of rocks
the crimson lorry moves at bicycle speed

Tonight, the moon will come out early
and the smell of piassava and palm kernel
will blend well with the aroma
from the Jange River

Hopscotch

I wish you were here
to throw pebbles into the air
and dip crumpled paper
into water flowing down the gutter

The marker you threw last night
landed squarely at the house we built
those sketches of chalk, of the mansion
that you created in your head next to mine

Let us go back to where we belong
underneath the breadfruit tree
where we took solace after a game
of hopscotch,
at the corner where everything grows.

Morning Cobwebs

My desire to dance along the riverbank
to the jaunty music of the Sewa
overtakes my uneasiness
and my wish to drift to safer grounds.

So, I watch the fisherman
as he lowers the landing net
at daybreak
and then ponder his catch at dusk.

Let us roll on the sand
among conch shells
like an unknown urchin
though I must admit
that the water around me
has grown against my stunted self.

The Dance

"Yo nunca habia bailado llegando aqui me han entusiasmado..."
"I have never danced, arriving here has enthused me..."
- Charanga Costena, Los Hermanos Flores

Take me to the middle of the road
to the center of the square
at the bridge where dust rises
and music resonates through walls

The sound from the flowing stream
against the uneven pillars
set my feet in frantic motion

It is with trepidation that I jump
into the shallow waterfall
to cleanse my unforgiving soul

Ha! The drumbeat for the *egugun*
catapults my feet into action
and a sudden feeling of resurrection
place me in a gratifying trance

Mystic Road

I have taken this road before
though I could not recall my way back

Along this path
I see a shrunken raggedy boy
carrying a crooked stick
with a red guillotine blade
branded on his left arm

Along this path
I see a girl with wobbly legs
and the reveler who blows smoke
on her sunken cheek
dance their worries away

my numbing toes could not keep up
with the ragtag militias
that ransack the village square

But the sun will come out another day
and the lives lost will be celebrated again.

Broken Canoe

I am the abandoned canoe
at the waterside
unclaimed and left to rot in the rain
brittle wood and wet termites
floating in my hollowed belly

Last night when the storm came
and I was hoping for my sail
to return to the raging sea
sand dunes held me back

But today
the tropical storm will return,
and I will fly away
on top of a mat that lay beside me.

Tropical Man

The sweat that drips steadily
down my oily face
represents my inner strength
to fight microbes
that penetrate my fettered feet

My senseless dreams dangle
minnows in mid air
with panoramic rings
and star-shaped dolls

bait is all I see on a rainy night

But my resilience is evident in candor
I speak truth to greybeards
and climb coconut trees
and then break nuts
with my bare hands

Scythe

The full moon
shone brightly last night
and the skeleton man
with the crimson scythe
walked in its shadow

Ant trail and coconut chaff
banana peel and slippery rocks
down the swampy path
with sharp edgy stones

Today we dare to dream
to confront the grim reaper
the one who grabs our soul
the crying baby's heart
and the feeble boy
who reaches for his drifting shoe.

We await the haunting cry
at the howling moon
and the frightening boy
and his wandering shoe
to return to the doorstep
of *Obatala's* shrine.

Owl

wide-eyed species that hoot at night

so they brought the pots, pans and drums
to chase away the bird that steals
the ailing kid who cries at night

women chanting, derriere exposed
the bird sat tight and gazed at me

drums and pans got louder still
at daylight's peak, the bird took heed
the women, they chased the culprit of doom
to yet another tree

The Haunting Cry

The deserted junction
awaits the haunting cry of an *orisha*

The voice of *Ogun* resonates
within the soul of the heartbroken
for he who breathes life into *ile aiye*
brings undying hope

He is the iron warrior
his dark steal hammer looms
to protect the heedless warrior
between the sea and the bushy hill

So, let us dance around a bonfire
let us trip on croaking frogs
with the chirping of birds
and the hissing of snakes
darkness is once again
giving way to life.

Winnows and Knotted Nets

White horses with wings
flying through blue smoke
an old woman carries within
her bosom a bundle of clothes
her eyes shut tightly
she is afraid of the night
while an old man waves
and then silently watches by
and with trembling hands
his eyes blinking fast
his little mongrel had fainted and died

A creature
steadily hops away
an elf-like man-beast
running toward the bay
he carries a ball pointed pen
he is clutching a bunch of keys
he hasn't washed his face in a while
and he totes a bag and a pocket knife
spitting kola chaffs, sipping homemade rum

White horses with wings
flying through blue smoke
women swing winnows
men with knotted nets
the old man won't drink
from this river again
with his eyes shut
and his head facing down

he will not dare to roam
for his fear is bigger
than his hunger and thirst

After the Rain

Last night the sky split open
and the grey running clouds collide
into a mighty thunderstorm

A melancholic breeze
blew past my house
as we wrapped tightly
underneath a wooden bed

After the rain
we witness an egret
on top of a grazing cow
feeding on crickets
butterflies and moths

After the rain
we watch a fluffy ball
float through the pungent air
from the huge cotton tree
at the bottom of the creek

Now the rushing clouds
have departed the naked sky
and the overflowing dam
no longer threatens the town

Seashore

I sit besides a palm tree
as my weariness amazes me
the breeze soothing my itchy skin

This warm saltwater flowing inland
has cured the fungal mess
between my twisted toes

So, let us dance to the wavy sound
of the blue water
let us sing to the tune
that she plays for me
my oily face bearing a smile

I was born walking
on eggshells and slime
my heels, on sharp edges of rocks
with yours next to mine

A Beautyful One

A child is born
with poetry tattooed on her forehead

In her mother's womb
she hears the call
of a hopeless society
of those that creep
through stained barbed wires
to fend for stale crumbs
and fragments of wheat
on the other side of the hill

So, she leaps from the belly of *Yemoja*
grabbing her crystalline beads on her way out.

Dawn

He toasts to the rise of dawn
with hardwood charcoal in his hand
thin ashes floating from the fireside
blue smoke forming a silhouette wall

The muezzin walks away from the tower
his voice rumbling through the morning air

He pauses, no state of hurriedness
to bear the burden of others and himself
he mutters the *shahada*
and returns to make the final call
his rasping voice piercing the masjid wall.

Green Hill

It is our innate instinct
to crawl underneath thorny plants
and wooden fences
to trade insult with the devil in the tunnel
beside the church where water flows.

Last night the water came gushing out
and my brother and his paper boat drifted away

But he was rescued
from the liquid spirit
by the pastor at the church
with the stained glass
the one who taught us to scream hallelujah
and then traded our effigy for a tiny cross.

A Beggar's Comet

We witness a beggar's blazing star
fall from the sky
we hear the distant thunder roar
and the sound of the bell toll
a solemn rendition of requiem

See the rumbling clouds crash
as the burning star nosedives
the heavens rain heavily
but the flares from his comet glows away

He leaves on his own terms
moans from men and ghosts
white horses and grazing cows
giving birth in the middle of town

So, let him take his royal bow
a transient on his way to the other side

Bondage

Son of Ham, in perpetual bondage
enslaved for his dark skin

So, we built the ark
that saved us from the flood
along the Odokoko river
we created the rainbow
then let the dove fly north
and the crow that you held in captivity

Heavy rock against my heaving heart
pain for rejecting to honor your gods

A crow will sing in the dead of night
a dove will return to its colorful nest
and the chains that held us bondage
shall be broken and made soft
freedom once again shall be free.

Lost in Juarez

She revels in the drizzling rain
against her window pane
reminding her of those misty nights
in paso del norte
many moons ago
alongside the Rio Grande

She slept underneath palm fronds
and bamboo sheets
moonlit sky, fireflies
and wet croaking frogs
far from the country
she called her home
a beautiful land
she named Sierra Leone

The coastal wave and the sea
the abandoned sea shells
and wild seaweeds
white sands drifting back
with the hasty wind
and the chihuahua sun
peeking through moving clouds

So now she wishes the heavy tide
that came in land,
that washed away the evil spirit
from that faraway town
where she buried a white cowry
and a withered plant
would return to cleanse her native land
land that she loves her Sierra Leone

Elegy for Alagba

Dust settles over an open field
near a stream in *Isale Eko*
where we lock arms in circles
by a fireside, and play a sad tune
a farewell song for a departing soul.

He who is gone but yet among us
who alters himself invincible
let him in one guttural note speak
to the town that offers sacrifice
that strikes the *bata* and chant his name

The *atokun* guides him around town
into the abyss of the Odokoko
where he returns to a land among men

Growing Shadows

The naked sun slowly moves
towards the middle of the sky
and the branches on the trees
form shadows
as we bask underneath
canopies of leaves

This is *Isale Eko*
where we gather
below stocky branches
of shadow spots, variegated leaves
and oozing sap
where we place our caps
over our dark oily faces

The image of the sun lingers
as we shut our eyes, as the sun
slowly creeps across our mental space

The Moon Rises

Palm fronds, green leaves and grass
and eyes floating in the dark

A grey ball in the sky
with a lone star guiding by
that we follow
into a haunted forest
where *Ogun* protects men

Let him tie an amulet on his *ibon*
and bear the cold winds
and prickled stems.
Let his guiding dogs
await in a roofless hut
as his tune travels the world

Tonight the moon will rise
over a town awaiting a hunter's return

In Shattered Glass

A broken rainbow buries itself
underneath a wooden bridge

a little man him plays a tune
for the girl who covers herself
in shattered glass and colorful paint

a tune that revives an ailing town
where debris float

she watches the wailing crowd
that sway to the tune of the wind
and the humming bird that sits on a rail

her smile returns to her tired face
as the *afere* blasts through the cement walls

Shadows On The Wall

The pregnant woman who sold nuts
on the cracked sidewalk
against her wishes
buries her head in the sand

Let her march through the old town
on gutter edges after the rain
hoping to be drifted away

For the storm that swept the town
twenty one days on end
took her bowlegged child away

A woman who sells groundnuts
counts shadows on a wall

Hodge-podge

I throw assortment of prayers on winnow
at the corner where four roads meet
as the tabernacle bells toll,
at midnight

My mind wanders into a future
of books and pillars of truths
mixed in a porridge bowl.

Let *Osun* drink
her wine, made from fermented stem
of cane-sugar and bitter kola nuts

Let her sail down the Odokoko
before we dump filth
under the wooden bridge
into the colorful freshwater,
that flows through the houses
on rickety posts

Do tears we amass
after the ritual dance
enough to bathe our unclean skin
after we lie prostrate for *Elegbara?*

Will the gourd we place
across our shoulders
contain a savory mix of soil and brine?

May the yolk that spill from the egg
from the hodge-podge at the junction,
be a sacrifice to those who left the land

Leicester Peak

I roam along a path, trowel in hand
wandering unto a bushy hillside
through prickly leaves and thorny weeds
trampled daisies on termite mounds
I lay my bag beside the rocky bank

It is a full moon night, fireflies fly high
tropical breeze blows hard on a humid night
I hum to the tune of a sparrow bird
far from the madness of the distant town

Thinking of the place that I left behind
where ants carry crumbs on their tiny backs

Her Dream (Young Eleanor)

She picks up the rice thrown at the bride
at the church where a wedding has been.
Melodic tune, white dress, a hunter's song
on a narrow street paved with sheep blood.
She sows seeds in her heart, nurtured bliss
in anticipation of a daring future,
of drizzling rain, from the holy water font
appeasing her soul in sudden readiness;
long after her sister was hurriedly slain
by a mother, underneath a coconut tree.
But for that joyful hymn, the organ call
at the beautiful church of Gibraltar
where melodies serenade the traders
that line the church walls.
Water flows against the house
with multiple heads
and the headscarves for the initiates,
stacked lace on satin, at the corner
with coral beads and her longing dream.

The Winding Road

In a distance I hear my name
called by the ghost who crosses
the road, carried by the wind

This never ending gravel street
treaded by wild ghouls and *witches*
rabid dogs and god horses

But freshwater stream alongside
with tombstones of those
who went before their time
and smoke from kerosene lamps

My name travels into eternity
down this winding road

Infuriation I

(Mount Aureol, Freetown Peninsula)

It is the audacity and callousness
Born out of a decomposed state of mind
Tearing apart a woven fabric of hope
It is the apathy of the educated few
The religiosity and feign optimism
And the calculated rationale of the elites
It is the noxious fumes suffocating the masses
Emitting from the flatulent exhaust of pigs
Parading the streets amid zombies and robots
It is the eerie silence of those who gain
From the status quo, the crumbs off the table
Of those who feast in decadence
It is the futility of hope, of courage betrayed
Of the refusal to speak truth to power
It is denial of the ominous signs and lessons
From yesterday's war, of the litany in history
That infuriates the crap out of me

Infuriation II

(Pademba Road Prison, Freetown)

It is the lawlessness in the streets
The evil and utter disregard
Of dark suited men in luxury cars
And the cliques in ominous alleys
That seamlessly blend love and hate
It is the pulpit call for the gallows
By those who wrote the books
That should be thrown at them,
Many times over
It is the calamity of being uprooted
By cranes, of twisted metals
And mangled piece,
A cry for rescue by onlookers
And pedestrians with cameras
Of riotous chants of frustration and anger
An image of blood, broken bones and pain
It is the apathy and the deafening silence
By those who are supposed to lead
That infuriates the crap out of me.

Infuriation III

The Other Marbella
(Costa del Sol -- Malaga, Spain)

It is the downpour on dirt roads and alleys
The overflowing streams at Susan's Bay
The coffee colored aqueous concoction
And the broken bottles and fecal mess
It is the clogged drain on the hillside
The storm that once cleansed our souls
Our possession of conjugated compost
It is the carcass of salmonella laden fowls
A desperate feast for the forsaken folk
The negligence, the apathy and greed
Of those who plant seeds that refuse to grow
And insist we wait for many moons to show
It is the deliberateness of their inaction
That infuriates the crap out of me.

A Sacred Heart

A parade for the martyrs
on a wet humid pre-easter night

Watch the four Castellanos
carry the Virgin Mary
on their broad shoulders

For this is a night in *Isale Eko*
when goblins and ghosts are wary
of the incense, from the choirboy
who marches in front of the line
along the potholed streets

So let us proceed to the cathedral
with the white priest
who taught us the catechism
and the nun who speaks in tongues
read the apostle's creed

A parade of worshippers
along a street littered with rosaries

The Rebirth of Isale Eko

Ogun retreats and sheathe his hammer
His weapon of truth, the one he wielded
When water splashes around the creek
The day the marauders invaded our town
And people run for the overlooking hills

He is our warrior king
The protector, our wing

He was *Tobe Ode*
Before coming to the creek
As he sprung out from the body of the queen

So, give him palm oil and chicken feet
Let us wipe our hands on his knees

Give him pounded yam and refried beans
For we welcome him home again
After the bloody battle is won

Give him ginger and kola nut
Let him spit the chaff at the junction
And into the mouth of the newborn
For life triumphs, and once again

Isale Eko celebrates him with drums

Change

When reticence is mistaken for idiocy
but the broken compass still points north

When the walls come caving down
but the songs of *Isale Eko* reverberate loudly

When silence is misread, indifference seized
and the resolve of man surges through

When vultures circle low for scavenging
and the smell of decay lingers on

Raging waters, muddy tires, clay toes and sweat
twisted metals, rusty knives, posters and phlegm

When grit stays strong, resilience a song
when the call from podium is the last word

When the little tent falls into the river
and change arrives, creeping, unnoticed

The trumpet stabbed the night in one last defiant note…

--Wole Soyinka

Forgiveness

As Ogun springs from the body of Yemeja
so is mercy that shower on *Isale Eko*
(along the stream where we bathe all night)

we wash our faces with tears of joy
the tears that roll after the mighty storm
the celebration, after the thunderous roar

Ha! Not long ago Ogun wept
the path we traverse was dark and muddy
the moon was red and deprived us,
the radiance of chiefs and the dead

the fire burns the shrub that cures
the path to manhood

for it is annihilation when kin destroy

the bond that fasten them
at the umbilicus
but we catapult
mercy, the town crier roars
as he beats his *ago-go*

as the rain pours at the doorstep of the healer

Isale Eko is re-born
peace is heard around the hills

the land where darkness once slept.

His Return

as darkness spreads over the quiet town
we hear the distant sound of
trumpet blaring across the land
and the late wind whispers goodbye
to sorrow

at *ile Isale Eko*, along the path to the two rivers
(where the battle was lost and won)
we celebrate his return
and dance the hunter's dance,

we paint our faces and collect cowries
a reminder of the sad yesteryears

Isale Eko is reborn
(the cry of joy again is heard)
and the newborn now has a name
the one who brought joy

did we shave his head and beat our drums
and throw away the remains of last night's *Sara*

Ha! the image of *Isale Eko*
the smell of daylight
the scent of joy
Kayode is home
again

Mosque of Cordoba

The naked moon is perched tonight
away from the dimly lit stars

Clusters of flycatcher birds
migrate over a minaret
erected on a hill
where scholars chant
while counting beads
around a stainless white sheet

They celebrate the *Mawlid*
while leaning on hypostyle pillars
underneath fragile metal fans
they recite verses from the gospel
a message of peace reverberated

The moon moves to the center sky
taking a single star as it travels by

Hurricane

Last night the howling wind
came back to tell the story
of a child who raised a storm
in a brass teacup

He flings walls of water inland
terrifying gusts with monstrous speed
as the crying stream echoes his call

We bid him farewell in a rickety boat
with a robe to wrap around his chest
and sprinkle gold dust on his way out

We tie an amulet on his oily ankles
and he travels the route of the slave ship
to the distant land where his forebear slept

So, with a christened name he lands
upon the plantation that they built
ripping the *uko* tree as he journeys inland

Down the Railway Line

Colorful prints, headscarves and beads
screaming women and cheerful kids
(The train is coming; the train is coming)
black smoke and fumes from engine pipes
ooh, the smell of spice and oil is rife
for burning noses and watery eyes

Take me back to the railway line
where traders hurriedly dress the ground
with clothes and food from faraway land
and fabrics waiting for the tailor's hands
I think of the red oily spill on the mats
of the old man who trades bitter kola nuts
I long for the days behind the curtain wall
where cobblers mend our battered shoes.
Let the screaming trader sell his books
and yell the names of *achebe, kongi* and *cole*
many pages reaped, missing covers and filth
highlighted paragraphs that we crave to read
tell the merchants who barter sugar for salt
and the little boy who sells his plastic bags
who jumps over the wares across the tracks
that the train is coming from the other side.

Owl

Wide-eyed species that hoot at night
so they brought the pots, pans and drums
to chase away the bird
that steals the ailing kid who cries at night
women chanting, derriere exposed
the bird sat tight and gazed at me
drums and pans got louder still
at daylight's peak, the bird took heed
the women, they chased the culprit of doom
to yet another tree

Morning

I listen to the croaking sound of the frogs
from underneath the rocks of worms
after the call for prayer is silenced
as the *ladani* walks away from the minaret
to perform his rakaats

Our metal containers pound on concrete
as I watch the wetness on the cracks
I force a smile and stretch my arms
to greet the new dawn

Desolation Road

Yesterday, wild wind and hurried rain
rushed past our wooden houses
standing on wobbly stilts

A drenching rain
leaving behind a sodden ground
of desolate land of butterflies

This is the road to wretchedness
where we gloss over cow dung
and leather skin

This is a path to nothingness
where thorns and dead roses
adorn a bridge hanging on faith

It is this road of barrenness
paved with a dream of hope
where we trade coconuts for books
to erase our mental anguish

The Bridge

a cave, decorated
with stalactites and stalagmites
where wet snails
are embedded in clayey rocks
and where cow skins
are soaked in burgundy dyes
all through the night.

the bridge will not fall tonight
but my heaving heart has melted away

across the stream
we follow the cow dung trail
while skipping through puddles
and dry excreta

tomorrow, the bridge will tremble and fall
and my feet will give way to the resonant force

Doorpost

He dares to think differently
so he prepares for aggression
by tying red ribbons and goat horns
and tiny cowries wrapped in black sateen
on his doorpost

Hallelujah and a *dua'* won't save him
when *Oluwa* comes to rescue him
at the fireside with blazing charcoals
where demons left his mortal flesh

Bring him water in a glass tumbler
and let him spill it at the entrance
give him a cow tail and fresh blood
to sprinkle on his floor and door knob

Daddy Ogboni shall sleep well tonight

Full Moon Rises

A naked moon rises over *Isale Eko*
and a dimly lit sunset faded
when the sweltering heat disappear.
I stand inside the mosque they burnt
on ageless mats where mortals kneel
to greet the night. Lantern and smoke
and prayer for she who lost a child
to the godforsaken barren land.
But the little boy who returns
with matchstick underneath his nails
as silence welcomes *Elegbara* again,
and the good-natured madman
who paints the sidewalk with facts
and an image of the immaculate sister
dance backwards to the waterfall
under full moon. Radiance, ash flakes
from the fire that lit the evening sky
where the full moon rises.

Antelope

The young child who serenades us
with a cheerful song
about the elusive antelope
reminds me of my lovely past

She turns her back
On the man who blows smoke
at the hunter with the hammer
and then runs into the field of ants

Let us cherish the dance
about the hunter that carries the *ibon*
along the path to the two rivers
in search of eternal peace

The Message

I have missions to accomplish
to gather and sow undesirable seeds
that fell among thorns and weeds

But let me swim among snails
upstream, where I will plant twigs
to grow far away from tweeting birds

When the days of harvesting is come
and canary birds sing the welcome song
my voice will echo through the valley floor

I have missions to accomplish
before the mighty storm rushes in

Tears

She will not lean against a cotton tree
until tears flow down her naked cheek
unto the nourished soil
where roses grow, allamanda for riches
and wreaths and garlands for the dead

For all her life, she awaits this moment
When wild horses gallop through town
to the other side, at *Ile Isale Ogede*
where umbilical cords are buried
underneath banana trees

Her hands gently weep
The redness of her eyes illuminate
corner street lamps, soot, black smoke
ballad for a reunion, a mother and child
as her tears vanish unto the earth

she leans on the ailing cotton tree
as *Oshun* disappears into her heart

Epiphany

Restless dogs, stray cats and bullets
a siege at the mouth of the atlantic
beyond a lion's roar. Lush greeneries
against incinerated metal fragments,
charred trees and burnt-out homes,
on granite on this day of epiphany.
It is a baptism of fire by night
engulfing a land built for freedom
and the magi who refuse to come.
It is at a doorstep of the temple
on the hill where we shout amen
and then inhale brown dust.
But from ashes to ashes, the wind
will help us breathe again
a fresh air for a fresh new year

Silent Soliloquy

I don't remember going home
my tired eyes refuse to close
endlessly I stand on the sidewalk
filthy water dowse my sweaty face

It is a day in my town
and my earpiece glued
to my earlobes,
with cords in pocket dangle
to honking vehicles passing by

I count colors as the cars go by
a kaleidoscope of life, a fancy sight
deafening cacophony freezing
my weary feet and my heart
thumping to the booming beat

This is Freetown
my very own town
that I never left in my mind
and in my soul
I carry you around
along the Guinea coast
across the ocean, in a rickety boat

This is my enclave
My ghetto, a *cidade da vida*
where traders fill my personal space
with smell of urine and spice
unclogging my nasal tracks

This is Freetown
in berets, straw hats and hijabs
and bald spots at the mercy
of the blazing sun
where in a potholed street,
and a pebble field
and my reflections display
on my polished boots

See a mad man with a whistle
as he rages on,
hear a song for the barefooted
and a ballad for a woman
who stutters my name out loud

But bright lights paint my evening sky
a roaring thunder and a rabid dog
shivers from underneath a trader's stall

The many people who walk by
melt into my darkness
but I don't remember going home
as my tired eyes refuse to close

Afterword

Lansana Gberie, PhD.

Ahmed Koroma begins his third poetry collection with a quotation from the legendary accordionist Salia Koroma (no relations): "I was present when lightning rent the sky at Ngeblama." It is a startling image, but it is not at odds with the general tone of nostalgia (or *'saudade'*) of the poems, fifty one in all. In the first and longest (661 words), "Dear Freetown," Koroma's mood of longing and melancholy, of a refusal to romanticise something about which he is so affectionate, is made clear. He is writing from a distance about a Freetown he left while still a young man, a Freetown that has changed radically, but a Freetown he insists must be shown in all its grits, its glories and its terrors. In his long absence, Freetown had suffered armed invasions, massive demographic changes, population explosion, had lost its once fabled placidity. Koroma does not yearn after that bucolic charm, doubting indeed whether there ever was one – "the pretense of a blissful town", he says. He yearns after an 'authentic' Freetown, "the battle scars down your tired face/reminding me of your stunning past."

When he returns to that city:

> *I want to be greeted by gentle fumes*
> *the smell of hot pepper soup on concrete*
> *mixed with odor of decayed compost*
> *sewage rats and roaming pigs*
> *I love you for who you are*

71

and for who you once were.

It is part of his great merit as a poet that Koroma commands many tones of voice. In his earlier paeans to the city he grew up in and loves – in the poems of *Along the Odokoko River (2016)* – the tone is lyrical, sometimes priapic, and finally elegiac. It was the voice of the child within the poet, the boy at home in his *isten* Freetown. In this new collection, Koroma's musings are sombre and melancholic, but he still manages to convey a longing, nostalgic mood. The musings seem very much like those of a middle-aged man finally deciding to return to that home after decades away. This accounts for the inchoate anxiety that suffuses these poems. When he returns, the poet says: "I do not want to be welcomed/with buntings, flags on crisscross wires/on steel poles and wooden fences." Rather

> *Place my picture next to the woman*
> *who spits at passersby*
> *in broad daylight*
> *let her scream my name out loud*
> *as my vehicle gallops through a heap*
> *of dirty rags.*

Is the poet laying it on too thick? Earlier poets of Freetown – Gladys Casely-Hayford, particularly – tended to idealise the city they so loved and missed, from a distance. Koroma takes a different approach, embracing everything, warts and all, and loving the stew. His are not the typical "nostalgia poetry": Koroma does not romanticise or idealise. Instead, he expresses his emotions without affectation, with no effort to induce starry-eyed emotions in the reader.

With the exception of "Dear Freetown," the poems in this collection are short to the point of terseness, the average length being around 75 words. Read together, however, they convey a powerful sense of authority and nuance: the voice is that of a mature craftsman at his peak. Koroma is unquestionably the best Sierra Leonean poet of his generation, a very thoughtful, conscientious and accomplished wordsmith.

The poems in this collection were written over a period of time, and the poetic sensibility fluctuates between longing, hope and outrage. In "Mystic Road," about terrorised villagers fleeing amidst the depredations of the civil war of the 1990s: the "numbing toes could not keep up/with the ragtag militias/that ransack the village square." There would be massacres, but the terror would pass. And "the sun will come out another day/and the lives lost will be celebrated again." Here, the poet, in spite of himself, confuses optimism – vacuous, unrealistic hectoring – with hope, which, as Terry Eagleton has reminded us, guards us against despair, and must be based upon realistic possibilities. The same sort of tendency is found in the "Dance", where "a sudden feeling of resurrection" places the poet in "a gratifying trance." In this state, one assumes, he encounters a derelict dugout – the title of the poem is "Broken Canoe" – but is held back from rowing away by the approaching tropical storm: to escape he "will fly away on top of a mat that lay besides me."

Hope and optimism, the magical flight of fancy, suddenly give way to three sources of 'infuriation' (the title for three poems at the end of the collection). The first is Mount Auroel, where Fourah Bay College sits on the Freetown Peninsula. The poet sees:

73

the audacity and callousness
Born out of a decomposed state of mind
Tearing apart a woven fabric of hope

And he muses about the:

the "futility of hope, of courage betrayed
Of the refusal to speak truth to power
It is denial of the ominous signs and lessons
From yesterday's war, of the litany in history
That infuriates the crap out of me."

A similar, more virulent infuriation is brought out of the poet
by the sight of Pademba Roads Prison and

"the lawlessness in the streets
The evil and utter disregard
Of dark suited men in luxury cars
And the cliques in ominous alleys
That seamlessly blend love and hate
It is the pulpit call for the gallows
By those who wrote the books
That should be thrown at them
Many times over."

Finally he encounters the notorious slum settlement of
Marbella. Out of his outrage emerges pure beauty, a fiercely
exact description of the settlement, literature:

It is the downpour on dirt roads and alleys
The overflowing streams at Susan's Bay
The coffee colored aqueous concoction

And the broken bottles and fecal mess
It is the clogged drain on the hillside
The storm that once cleansed our souls
Our possession of conjugated compost
It is the carcass of salmonella laden fowls
A desperate feast for the forsaken folk
The negligence, the apathy and greed
Of those who plant seeds that refuse to grow
And insist we wait for many moons to show
It is the deliberateness of their inaction
That infuriates the crap out of me.

In Koroma's company, poetry becomes both a source of real pleasure, and a prick on the conscience. He lets you see, and he nudges you to act. For that, he will be read for long.